The
Patrol Leader
Handbook

BOY SCOUTS OF AMERICA®

32502A
ISBN 0-8395-2502-8
©2005 Boy Scouts of America

Contents

1

Opportunity and Challenge

Welcome to
the Position of
Patrol Leader

1

Opportunity and Challenge— Welcome to the Position of Patrol Leader

Congratulations!

The members of your patrol have elected you to be their leader. They've given you a pat on the back, put their trust in you, and wished you good luck.

You have just received one of the best positions in Scouting. It will be challenging, exciting, and sometimes perhaps a little frustrating, but as you explore ways to lead the members of the patrol, you will discover the many rewards of being a patrol leader. You will learn a great deal and have plenty of fun. Along the way, you will enjoy some of the most satisfying experiences of Scouting.

The patrol will look to you for guidance. The Scoutmaster and other troop leaders expect you to do your best. They want you to be successful, so you can expect their help as well. You want to be the most effective patrol leader you can be.

You were elected because your fellow Scouts trust you and believe that you will help the troop be successful and help them have a better Scouting experience. Good leaders accept leadership roles because they want to make a difference. Good leaders are servant leaders. They focus on helping others succeed.

Perhaps you are a little nervous about how you will fulfill your new responsibilities. You may be unsure of exactly what to do and when. Those are reasonable concerns. Most new patrol leaders have them. They are signs that you care about the patrol and the troop, and that you want to do your best.

Are you ready to get started? Then let's begin.

First Things First

Have confidence that leading a patrol is a responsibility that you can handle. Yes, you are a new patrol leader, but you are also the same person you were before you were elected. Members of your patrol saw something in you that convinced them you would be a good leader. You probably have many leadership skills already, even if you have not had many chances to use them, and you probably have many questions about your new position. This handbook will help you learn what it takes to be a great patrol leader.

What Is Expected of Me?

While you are a patrol leader, your troop and patrol are going to count on you to live up to some clear expectations. They will look to you to:

- Represent the patrol at all patrol leaders' council meetings and the annual program planning conference.

- Keep patrol members informed of decisions made by the patrol leaders' council.

- Play a key role in planning, leading, and evaluating patrol meetings and activities.

- Help the patrol prepare to participate in all troop activities.

- Learn about the abilities of other patrol members and fully involve them in patrol and troop activities by assigning them specific tasks and responsibilities.

- Attend troop leadership training and continue to work on advancement.

- Encourage patrol members to complete their own advancement requirements.

- Set a good example by having a positive attitude, wearing the Scout uniform, showing patrol spirit, and expecting the best from yourself and others.

- Devote the time necessary to be an effective leader.

- Work with others in the troop to make the troop go.

- Live by the Scout Oath and Law.

- Solicit ideas and concerns from patrol members so they have input to the planning and operation of the patrol.

What Tools Do I Have?

The Boy Scouts of America would not expect you to accept the responsibilities of being a patrol leader without providing you with the resources you need to succeed. The following are a few items you will find in your leadership tool chest:

Introduction to Leadership Training

Soon after you become a patrol leader, your Scoutmaster will schedule an introductory meeting to help you get a good start at being an effective leader. The session may include a small group of other troop leaders and probably will last about an hour. No doubt your Scoutmaster will express pleasure in having you as a patrol leader and will remind you how important your contribution to the troop will be.

This meeting with your Scoutmaster may also cover specific leadership suggestions for upcoming patrol meetings and activities. Expect to learn about the ways troop leaders will support you and provide guidance, and where you can find other BSA resources of value to patrol leaders.

Troop Leadership Training

The Troop Leadership Training workshop will be held soon after your election and will involve all the troop's youth leaders. It consists of three hour-long modules that cover the basics of what a youth leader must *Be*, what he must *Know*, and what he must *Do*. It is designed to answer three basic questions:

- What is my role?
- What does success look like in my role?
- What is expected of me?

The objective of Troop Leadership Training is to give you a clearer picture of how your position fits in the troop and how you can make a difference.

Scouting Literature

The Patrol Leader Handbook you are holding is one of the most useful leadership tools available to you. As you read through this handbook, you will discover that other publications, such as the *Boy Scout Handbook, Fieldbook,* and other Scouting manuals, also can be helpful.

Other Patrol Leaders

As a member of a patrol, you probably have seen other Scouts serving as patrol leaders. As the leader of one of the patrols making up a troop, you will be working alongside several other current patrol leaders. Their successful methods of leadership can serve as examples of what may work for you, too. Feel free to ask experienced patrol leaders how they handle different situations.

Other Patrol Members

Patrol members can be tremendous sources of information, energy, and enthusiasm. Listen to them carefully. Find out what they are thinking and how they would like the patrol to operate, then involve them in planning and carrying out the patrol's meetings and activities.

Other Troop Leaders

The most experienced leaders of a troop are the Scoutmaster, assistant Scoutmasters, and senior patrol leader. All of them can offer guidance and support as you learn how to lead. If you are the patrol leader of a new-Scout patrol, you probably will have a troop guide to help you every step of the way. Also, your troop may have older Scouts serving as instructors and junior assistant Scoutmasters who can lend a hand.

As a patrol leader, you can depend upon other leaders of the troop to support you in the following ways:

- They will be available to help answer your questions.

- They will provide direction, coaching, support, and opportunities for leadership training and development.

- They will listen to your ideas.

- They will be fair.

- They will serve as good examples.

- If you ask for it, they will offer advice.

- They will back you on reasonable leadership decisions.

How Will I Know I Am Leading Well?

As a patrol leader, you will encounter many situations. Sometimes it will seem as if everything your patrol tries goes exactly right— the weather for a campout is perfect, patrol meals cooked over camp stoves are tasty and filling, and everybody has a good time taking part in the patrol's activities.

However, there will be moments when it all seems to be falling apart. A patrol event may be dampened by bad weather. Patrol members may forget essential gear. Spirits may be down and energy low.

Through good times and bad, the first clue that you are leading well is that you are doing your best. You are using the knowledge you have and the resources around you to help the patrol find a good way through any situation. By staying cheerful and by always looking for solutions to problems confronting the patrol, you will set an example for others. That sort of leadership can get a patrol through the toughest challenges.

It is a good idea to sit down with patrol members at the end of an activity and take a few minutes to talk about recent events. You can learn a great deal about the success of an event and about your leadership role by reflecting on some or all of the following questions:

- In what ways did things go as our patrol expected? In what ways did they not?

- How good was our planning and preparation? What could we do better next time?

- What did patrol members like best about this experience? What would they change next time?

- What did we learn during this event?

- As we prepare for future events, what are some of the ways we can make our patrol even better?

Tips to Get You Started

There are lots of ways to be a good patrol leader. Over time, you will learn many of them. Adult leaders, the senior patrol leader, and other patrol leaders will help you put effective leadership methods into practice. On your own, you will learn much about leading through trial and error.

All of that will take time, of course. The following tips can help you lead the patrol right from the start:

- **Keep your word.** Don't make promises you can't—or don't intend to—keep.

- **Be fair to all.** A good leader shows no favorites. Don't allow friendships to stand in the way of treating all members of the patrol equally. Know who likes to do what, and try to assign responsibilities to Scouts according to their interests.

- **Communicate.** A good leader knows how to get and give information so that everyone understands. You don't need a commanding voice to be a good leader, but you do need to be a good listener. Relating to the members of your patrol will help you guide them in the right direction. Understand the value of asking questions to guide the audience. Questions help the listener understand better and formulate his or her own thoughts, ideas, and solutions.

- **Be flexible.** Meetings, campouts, and other patrol events will not always go as planned. Be open to new opportunities, and be willing to shift to a backup plan if original expectations change.

- **Be organized.** Time spent preparing for patrol meetings and events will be repaid many times over. At patrol meetings, record who agrees to do each task. Fill out the duty roster before going on a campout.

- **Delegate.** One of the greatest strengths of a good leader is the willingness to empower others to accomplish all they can. Most people like to be challenged. Encourage your patrol members to do things they can do well and to increase their knowledge and confidence by taking on tasks they have never tried before.

- **Set the example.** Whatever you do, your patrol members are likely to do the same. Lead by example in your attitude, your relationships with others, and your approach to leading the patrol.

- **Be consistent.** Nothing is more confusing for a group than a leader who is one way one moment and the opposite a short time later. When your patrol members know what to expect from you, they will be more likely to respond positively to your leadership.

- **Give praise.** Offer honest praise whenever you can. Simply saying, "Nice job!" can go a long way toward making a Scout feel he is contributing to the effort of the patrol. Good leaders know that the best way to get credit is to keep giving it away.

- **Ask for help.** Don't be embarrassed to ask questions or to draw on the many resources available to you. When confronted with a situation you don't know how to handle, or just to get another opinion on a plan that seems to be going well, ask experienced troop leaders for guidance and advice.

- **Have fun.** Learning to be a good leader is an important part of the adventure of Scouting. Much of what you do as a patrol leader will be very successful, but sometimes you will discover that certain leadership approaches you try don't work so well. Keep trying, though, and give it your best effort. Most of all, have fun learning to be a leader. Your joy and enthusiasm will spread to other Scouts and can energize the activities of your patrol.

Your Patrol (Draw your patrol symbol here.)

This form provides spaces for vital information about troop leadership and the members of your patrol. Fill it out completely and keep it handy to increase communication.

Patrol Members

Name	Address		
E-mail	Telephone	Rank	Patrol position

Name	Address		
E-mail	Telephone	Rank	Patrol position

Name	Address		
E-mail	Telephone	Rank	Patrol position

Name	Address		
E-mail	Telephone	Rank	Patrol position

Name	Address		
E-mail	Telephone	Rank	Patrol position

Name	Address		
E-mail	Telephone	Rank	Patrol position

Troop Leaders

Scoutmaster   Address

    E-mail   Telephone

Senior patrol leader   Address

    E-mail   Telephone

Troop guide   Address

    E-mail   Telephone

Assistant Scoutmaster   Address

    E-mail   Telephone

Assistant Scoutmaster   Address

    E-mail   Telephone

Patrol leader   Address

    E-mail   Telephone

Patrol leader   Address

    E-mail   Telephone

Patrol leader   Address

    E-mail   Telephone

Patrol leader   Address

    E-mail   Telephone

Name _____

What does success look like for our troop? _____

_____

_____

_____

_____

_____

_____

_____

_____

What are my goals to get us there? _____

_____

_____

_____

_____

_____

_____

_____

_____

_____

_____

Building
Patrol Spirit

Building Patrol Spirit

Scout Spirit and Patrol Spirit

Patrol spirit, like Scout spirit, has as its foundation the Scout Oath and Law. Patrol spirit also builds on the bonds of friendship among a small group of Scouts who share the common goal of making their patrol the best it can be.

Check the requirements

for any Boy Scout rank and you'll find that Scouts are expected to demonstrate "Scout spirit." You probably already know that you show Scout spirit when you live according to the Scout Oath and Law, when you are prepared for anything that comes along, and when you are willing to give time and energy to support and improve your troop, your community, and your nation.

As a patrol leader, you are also expected to show "patrol spirit." Patrol spirit is similar to Scout spirit, but instead of focusing on your troop, the spotlight is on the group of friends you know as members of your patrol. All of you can demonstrate patrol spirit by working together toward the common goal of building the very best possible patrol. As the leader of the patrol, you can play a key role in helping the patrol achieve all it can.

Much of the spirit of your patrol will be shaped by the experiences that you and other patrol members share. A weekend camping trip, a terrific day of canoeing on a quiet river, a service project to repair community buildings, a patrol meeting full of laughter and progress—everything that you do as a group will pull your patrol together and give it a history all its own.

The misadventures of a patrol can be just as valuable in building patrol spirit as can the successes. A patrol that draws on all its resources to deal with a storm in the backcountry, a community event that isn't going well, or the struggles of a patrol member trying to learn certain advancement skills can increase the closeness of a patrol and make Scouting an even more valuable experience for everyone.

In addition to shared experiences, the patrol has a number of other ways to help build patrol spirit. Among them are the patrol's name, flag, yell, song, meeting place, gear, and specialties. Also important will be activities involving the patrol with other patrols and with the entire troop.

Your Patrol's Name

A good name sets your patrol apart from all others and provides patrol members with a special way of identifying themselves. In some troops, patrol names that are deeply rooted in tradition are passed down from one generation of Scouts to the next. In other troops, Scouts forming new patrols are invited to choose names they feel are just right for them.

Since the earliest days of Scouting, patrols have looked to wildlife and to forests for name ideas. Does your patrol love to roam? Perhaps you will become the Buffalo Patrol. Are patrol members strong swimmers? Maybe Shark Patrol is an appropriate name. If patrol members are committed to rising above it all, you might call yourselves the Pine Tree Patrol. You can even spice up your patrol's name with a descriptive word— Soaring Hawk Patrol, for example, or the Leaping Lizards.

Patrol Emblems

The BSA's Supply Division has patrol
emblems for a wide variety of names.
Blank emblems also are available for
patrols wishing to design their own.
The patrol emblem is worn on the
right sleeve of the Boy Scout uniform.

Your Patrol's Flag

The trademark of your patrol is its flag, and it should be a good one. Patrol members can put their heads together to design a flag that features the patrol's emblem and additional decorations that show something about the patrol. Make the flag out of canvas or other heavy cloth, and use permanent markers or paint to embellish it. Include your troop number and the names of all members of the patrol. Add ribbons, streamers, and other awards that the patrol earns during Scouting events. Then mount the flag on a pole and carry it wherever the patrol goes.

Your Patrol's Yell and Song

Go to any Scouting event and you may hear the shrill cry of the Eagle Patrol, the growl of the Grizzly Patrol, and the hoot of the Owl Patrol. Every patrol should have a yell. Make yours short, snappy, and somehow related to the name and identity of the patrol. Use the patrol yell to announce to the other patrols that your patrol is ready to go, is present during a troop assembly, or has done well during a patrol game.

How about a patrol song or chant? Draw on the creative powers of the patrol members to come up with new words to an old song or to invent a short, catchy chant that describes your patrol's strengths.

Your Patrol's Meeting Place and Gear

Over time, your patrol may build up a collection of camping gear and other items set aside for use by patrol members. Keeping track of everything is important, especially when the gear of several patrols becomes mixed together on a campout or during troop events.

A good way to organize patrol equipment and to display patrol spirit is to mark items with the patrol emblem. Mark small items by using permanent ink to draw an outline of the patrol emblem, or use a rubber stamp that features the emblem. For larger items such as a chuck box, consider using a stencil of the emblem and spray paint.

If your patrol has a meeting place of its own—a corner of the troop meeting room, for example—encourage patrol members to decorate it to reflect the identity of the patrol. Build on the theme of your patrol name. For instance, the Bear Patrol could develop their meeting area into "The Bears' Den" while the Raven Patrol fixes up a space they call "Ravens' Nest."

Your Patrol's Specialties

Does your patrol have a specialty? Perhaps patrol members are especially good at baking cobblers during campouts or making mouth-watering stew. Maybe patrol members especially like to hike, use maps and compasses, bicycle, or make music together.

During your time as a patrol leader, you can encourage members of your patrol to practice their specialties and to learn new ones. Working as a group, you can become known as a patrol that knows how to take care of itself in the backcountry, how to repair eroded trails, or how to do any of a hundred other skills.

Your Patrol's Activities

Most patrol activities take place within the framework of the troop. However, patrols may also set out on day hikes, service projects, and overnighters independent of the troop and free of adult leadership as long as they follow two rules:

- The Scoutmaster approves the patrol activity.
- The patrol activity does not interfere with any troop function.

A patrol activity without adult supervision should be allowed only when it has been thoroughly planned and the Scoutmaster is satisfied the activity is well within patrol members' levels of training and responsibility. If the Scoutmaster has any doubts, he should encourage the patrol to reconsider its plans or should assign adults to accompany the patrol during the activity.

Patrol Competitions

A patrol is a team of friends. A natural interest of any team is to test itself, using the skills and abilities of everyone in the group to overcome challenges. The interpatrol activities that occur at most troop meetings offer an ideal setting for your patrol to take part in contests and competitions. In addition to being enjoyable, these events will help your patrol strengthen the bonds of friendship and cooperation that hold it together.

Led by the senior patrol leader or by someone assigned to the task, an interpatrol activity may be a game that tests the skills Scouts are learning for an upcoming activity. For example, it might be a race by the patrols to set up tents properly or a relay in which all members of each patrol correctly tie a set of knots. Other possibilities include:

- Compass bearing walk
- Knot-tying relay
- Nature scavenger hunt
- Bow-saw relay
- Wet-weather fire building contest
- String burning race
- Flagpole raising contest

Some games require quickness while others depend on knowledge. Many of Scouting's initiative games have no winners or losers, but instead encourage patrols to cooperate as teams to solve problems.

Competition and the Scouting Program

Scouting offers patrol members many opportunities to take part in competitions. Some will encourage Scouts to use Scouting skills, while others will ask patrol members to work together to succeed. Now and then, a competition will be a game or activity designed simply for patrols to have fun. Whatever forms they take, competitions in Scouting should do the following:

- Increase the confidence and self-esteem of every Scout.

- Increase mutual support among members of patrols and troops.

- Contribute to group decision-making and leadership.

- Increase the members' abilities in mutual planning and problem solving.

The National Honor Patrol Award

The National Honor Patrol Award is presented to patrols whose members have gone all out to build the best patrols possible. Members can earn the award for their patrol by fulfilling the following requirements over a three-month period:

1. Have a patrol name, flag, and yell. Put the patrol design on equipment and use the patrol yell. Keep patrol records up-to-date.

2. Hold two patrol meetings every month.

3. Take part in at least one hike, outdoor activity, or other Scouting event.

4. Complete two Good Turns or service projects approved by the patrol leaders' council.

5. Help two patrol members advance one rank.

6. Wear the full uniform correctly at troop activities. (To complete this requirement, at least 75 percent of the patrol's membership must be in uniform.)

7. Have a representative attend at least three patrol leaders' council meetings.

8. Have eight members in the patrol, or experience an increase in patrol membership.

3

Your Patrol and Your Troop

Your Patrol and Your Troop

Robert Baden-Powell, the founder of Scouting, said, "The patrol method is not a way to operate a Boy Scout troop, it is the only way. Unless the patrol method is in operation you don't really have a Boy Scout troop."

If you're going to lead a patrol, it's a good idea to know exactly what a patrol is. Here's how *The Scoutmaster Handbook* defines it:

> Patrols are the building blocks of a Boy Scout troop.
> A patrol is a small group of boys who are more or
> less similar in age, development, and interests.
> Working together as a team, patrol members share
> the responsibility of making the patrol a success.
> They gain confidence by serving in positions of
> patrol leadership. All enjoy the
> friendship, sense of belonging,
> and achievements of the patrol
> and of each of its members.
>
> —*The Scoutmaster Handbook*

Your patrol is one of several that make up the troop. Just as each patrol member plays an important role in the success of the patrol, each patrol is essential for making the troop go. Take a look at a troop organization chart and you can see that patrols are the building blocks of a troop.

Sample Youth Leader Organizational Chart for a Large Troop

In this sample, there are enough members to fill all of the patrols and leadership positions.

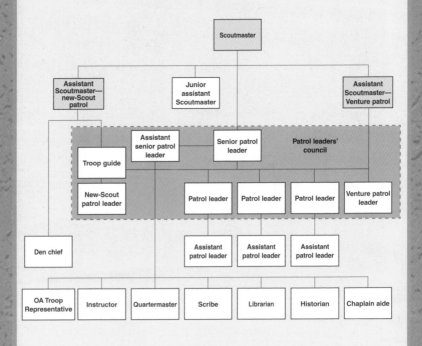

Sample Youth Leader Organizational Chart for a Small Troop

As more boys join, more patrols can be formed and more leadership positions filled.

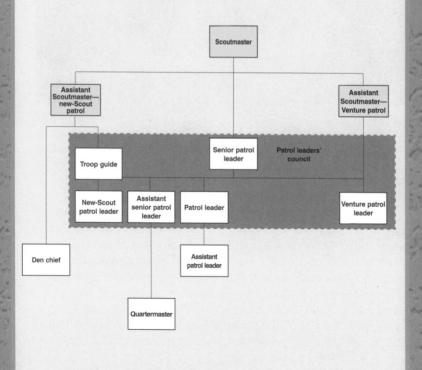

The number of Scouts in a patrol depends upon a troop's total enrollment and the needs of its members. Ideally, each patrol will have eight members. Troop members can help smaller patrols get up to full strength by encouraging friends and classmates to join the troop and take part in the Scouting program.

A patrol elects one of its members to be the patrol leader to provide the members with guidance and to represent them on the patrol leaders' council. The qualifications required of patrol leader candidates (age, rank, etc.) are determined by each troop. Most troops hold patrol leader elections twice a year, though some may have elections more often. The voting process is usually done by secret ballot. Upon election, the patrol leader then appoints members of the patrol to fill other patrol leadership positions that may include assistant patrol leader, quartermaster, grubmaster, and cheermaster.

Three Types of Patrols

A troop usually consists of three types of patrols:

❶ New-Scout patrols

❷ Regular patrols

❸ Venture patrols

New-Scout Patrols

New-Scout patrols are for younger Scouts who have recently joined a troop. They will stay together as members of a new-Scout patrol for their first year as Boy Scouts. Each new-Scout patrol has an older, experienced Scout called a *troop guide* to help the patrol members through the challenges of troop membership. An assistant Scoutmaster also can assist the new-Scout patrol to be sure that youth beginning the adventure of Boy Scouting get off to a good start.

The new-Scout patrol elects a patrol leader just as the other patrols do. To give more members of the new-Scout patrol the opportunity to gain leadership experience, new-Scout patrol leaders may serve for a shorter period of time than the leaders of regular patrols.

Regular Patrols

Regular patrols are for Scouts who have been in a troop for at least a year and have completed, or are close to completing, the requirements for the First Class rank. These are Scouts who have been around the BSA long enough to be comfortable with the patrol and troop operation, and who are experienced in Scouting's outdoor skills. Each regular patrol elects its own patrol leader. Regular patrols may plan patrol activities independent of the troop, such as a hike or a service project, with approval of the Scoutmaster.

Venture Patrols

Venture patrols are made up of Scouts who are at least 13 years old and have exhibited the maturity and skills to take on more challenging activities than those available to a troop's less experienced members. While a portion of a troop attends resident summer camp, for example, a Venture patrol may set out on a high-adventure activity.

Members of Venture patrols continue to function as a patrol within the troop. They elect a patrol leader, and they may hold troop leadership positions. An assistant Scoutmaster who enjoys high-adventure activities provides guidance and mentoring for the Venture patrol, helps members plan upcoming activities, and coordinates their roles as key players in troop meetings, instruction, and events. Venture patrol members

wear the Scout uniform with the Venture strip above the right pocket. The Venture patrol leader wears the same patrol leader patch as the troop's other patrol leaders.

As may be expected, the Venture patrol leader often has more responsibilities than the leaders of new-Scout patrols or regular patrols. A Venture patrol moves at a faster pace than do other patrols, and its activities are more demanding. A Venture patrol leader will work in cooperation with the Scoutmaster, senior patrol leader, and one or more assistant Scoutmasters to help his patrol put together the pieces for upcoming adventures and to serve as skills instructors and participants in troop meetings and other troop activities.

The leaders of Venture patrols will find plenty of great ideas for their patrols in the three volumes of the BSA publication *Varsity/Venture Program Features,* Nos. 34837, 34838, and 34839. The volumes offer more than two dozen fully developed plans for programs involving exciting high-adventure and sport activities.

The Senior Patrol Leader

Just as the patrol leader is the leader of patrol members, the senior patrol leader is the leader of the troop. The senior patrol leader is responsible for the troop's overall operation. With guidance from the Scoutmaster, he takes charge of troop meetings, of the patrol leaders' council, and of all troop activities, and he does everything he can to help each patrol be successful. He is responsible for annual program planning conferences and assists the Scoutmaster in conducting the troop leadership training. The senior patrol leader presides over the patrol leaders'

council and works closely with each patrol leader to plan troop meetings and make arrangements for troop activities.

All members of a troop vote by secret ballot to choose their senior patrol leader. Rank and age requirements to be a senior patrol leader are determined by each troop, as is the schedule of elections. During a Scout's time as senior patrol leader, he is not a member of any patrol but may participate with a Venture patrol in high-adventure activities.

Senior Patrol Leaders of the Future

Most senior patrol leaders have previously served as patrol leaders. They have learned how to manage patrol and troop meetings, projects, and activities. As a patrol leader yourself, you are gaining the expertise that will be helpful if your fellow Scouts one day elect you to be the troop's senior patrol leader.

The relationship of the senior patrol leader and the Scoutmaster should be one of mutual friendship and admiration. You'll see this displayed before every meeting of the troop as the senior patrol leader and the Scoutmaster review the agenda. You can expect to see them together again at the conclusion of the meeting, discussing how everything went and what adjustments or assignments should be made before the troop's next activity.

Other Troop Leadership Positions

Different troops have different leadership needs. With the guidance and approval of the Scoutmaster, the senior patrol leader determines which positions will most benefit the troop, then he selects the Scout who will hold each of those positions. With the exception of assistant senior patrol leader and troop guide, Scouts filling all the other troop positions will continue to be active members of their patrols. In addition to the troop positions described in this chapter, Scouts may be appointed by their patrol leaders to serve in certain patrol leadership positions.

Assistant Senior Patrol Leader

The senior patrol leader appoints the assistant senior patrol leader with the approval of the Scoutmaster. Among the assistant senior patrol leader's specific duties are providing training and guidance for the troop's quartermaster, scribe, Order of the Arrow representative, historian, librarian, and instructors. He serves in place of the senior patrol leader at meetings and events when the senior patrol leader must be absent.

The assistant senior patrol leader is not a member of a patrol but may take part in the activities of a Venture patrol. Large troops may have more than one assistant senior patrol leader.

Troop Guide

Each new-Scout patrol in a troop should have its own troop guide. A troop guide is an older Scout who holds the rank of First Class or higher, has strong teaching skills, and possesses the patience to work with new Scouts. As a mentor to the patrol leader of the new-Scout patrol, he provides direction for the patrol leader and helps him with his patrol leader responsibilities. The troop guide accompanies the new-Scout patrol on troop campouts and makes himself available to assist the new Scouts as they learn fundamental Scouting skills. He usually is not a member of another patrol, but he may participate in the high-adventure activities of a Venture patrol. Along with the patrol leader of the new-Scout patrol, he is a member of the patrol leaders' council.

Quartermaster

The quartermaster is the troop's supply boss. He keeps an inventory of troop equipment and sees that the gear is in good condition. He works with patrol quartermasters as they check out equipment and return it, and at meetings of the patrol leaders' council reports on the status of equipment in need of replacement or repair. In carrying out his responsibilities, he may have the guidance of a member of the troop committee.

Troop Scribe

The scribe is the troop's secretary. He keeps the minutes of the patrol leaders' council meetings but is not a voting member of the council. The scribe may also keep attendance records of other troop activities, such as campouts and service projects. During troop meetings, he works with patrol scribes to ensure the accurate recording of attendance and payment of dues, and to keep advancement records up-to-date.

The scribe may also be responsible for maintaining a troop Web site with information that is current and correct. An adult who is a member of the troop committee may be assigned to help the troop scribe carry out his responsibilities.

Troop Order of the Arrow Representative

An Order of the Arrow representative can be appointed by the senior patrol leader to be a link between the troop and the local Order of the Arrow lodge. By enhancing the image of the Order as a service arm to the troop, the representative promotes the OA, urges troop members to take part in resident camping, and encourages older Scouts to seek out opportunities for high adventure. The OA representative assists with leadership skills training in the troop and supports fellow Arrowmen undertaking unit leadership roles. He reports to the assistant senior patrol leader.

Troop Historian

The troop historian collects and preserves troop photographs, news stories, trophies, flags, scrapbooks, awards, and other memorabilia. He may also gather and organize information about the troop's former members and leaders, and make those materials available for Scouting activities, media contacts, and troop history projects. Troop displays prepared by the historian can be used during courts of honor, troop open houses, and other special Scouting occasions.

Troop Librarian

The troop librarian oversees the care and use of troop books, merit badge pamphlets, magazines, audiovisuals, diskettes, and lists of merit badge counselors. He checks out these materials to Scouts and leaders and maintains records to ensure that all items are returned. He may also suggest the purchase of new literature and report the need to repair or replace any current items.

Instructor

Each instructor is an older troop member who is proficient in Scouting skills and has the ability to teach those skills to others. The subjects that instructors may wish to teach include any of the areas that Scouts want to master, especially those such as first aid, camping, backpacking, orienteering, and others required for outdoor activities and rank advancement. A troop may have more than one instructor.

Chaplain Aide

The chaplain aide assists the troop chaplain (an adult from the troop committee or the chartered organization) in conducting the troop's religious observances. He sees that religious holidays are considered during program planning, and he promotes the religious emblems program.

Den Chief

A den chief works with a den of Cub Scouts and with their adult leader. He assists with den meetings, encourages Cub Scout advancement, and serves as a role model for younger boys. Being a den chief can be a great first leadership experience for a Scout. Depending on the number of dens in the Cub Scout packs of its community, a troop may have several members serving as den chiefs. Den chiefs can be a great asset to den leaders and are deeply appreciated and admired by Cub Scouts and Cub Scout leaders alike.

Webelos Den Chief

A Webelos den chief meets each week with a Webelos den and helps its adult leader guide the Webelos Scouts to make the most of their program. He can assist with den meetings and activities, lead songs and games, and encourage Webelos Scouts to look forward to the adventure of Boy Scouting that awaits them when they are old enough to join the troop.

Junior Assistant Scoutmaster

A Scout at least 16 years of age who has shown outstanding leadership skills may be appointed by the senior patrol leader, with the consent of the Scoutmaster, to serve as a junior assistant Scoutmaster. A junior assistant Scoutmaster follows the guidance of the Scoutmaster in providing support and supervision to the troop's other boy leaders. He can be a valuable resource for teaching Scouting skills to younger Scouts and in providing leadership to the troop. Upon turning 18, a junior assistant Scoutmaster is eligible to become an assistant Scoutmaster. A troop may have more than one junior assistant Scoutmaster.

The Patrol Leaders' Council

An important goal of Boy Scouting is that troops are Scout-planned and Scout-led. That means that the Scouts themselves accept responsibility for putting together an exciting and challenging program for a troop and then seeing that it becomes a reality. The patrol leaders' council (also known as the PLC) is the mechanism by which a troop's program is planned by its members and put into action.

The patrol leaders' council is made up of the following troop members:

- The senior patrol leader, who presides over the PLC

- The assistant senior patrol leader

- Patrol leaders of each patrol, including the new-Scout patrol and the Venture patrol

- Troop guides

- Troop scribe, who records the minutes of the meeting but is not a voting member of the council

- Other troop leaders, as needed

Meetings of the Patrol Leaders' Council

The patrol leaders' council plans the yearly troop program at an annual program planning conference. It then meets every four weeks to fine-tune the plans for the coming month.

At the conclusion of troop meetings (and at other times the senior patrol leader feels the PLC should consider an issue) the council meets informally (a "stand-up meeting") to review the success of a troop activity and to go over responsibilities for future meetings and events.

The Scoutmaster attends PLC meetings in a supportive role to provide information and insight on issues and activities. To the greatest extent possible, the members of the patrol leaders' council plan and carry out the program of a Scout-run, Scout-led troop.

In addition to program planning, the patrol leaders' council may deal with other issues concerning the troop and its members:

- Advancement needs
- Special awards
- Fund-raising projects
- Good Turn programs
- Conservation projects
- Special programs with the chartered organization
- Scout Sunday, Sabbath, and Scouting Anniversary Week
- Recruitment plans
- Webelos-to-Scout transition
- Special ceremonies
- Community events such as parades and festivals
- Disciplinary issues

Members of a troop's patrol leaders' council can expect to meet in three different ways:

- Annual program planning conference
- Monthly PLC meetings
- Stand-up PLC meetings before and after troop activities

Annual Program Planning Conference

During an annual program planning conference, members of the patrol leaders' council—not the adult leaders—are responsible for planning troop activities. The senior patrol leader and the Scoutmaster then present the new annual plan to the troop committee for its support. If revisions are suggested, the senior patrol leader will consult with the patrol leaders' council to make appropriate changes.

The conference is a time for members of the PLC to work through the details of a program, find any flaws, and make certain the possibilities being considered for the troop are exciting, challenging, worthwhile, and practical. Before finalizing a program plan, the council will consider factors including costs, logistics, and the skill levels of troop members. In the role of a guide and supporter, the Scoutmaster may occasionally step in to raise important questions or steer the discussion in a new direction.

The senior patrol leader chairs the conference. He works closely with the Scoutmaster before the conference to finalize the conference location, meal plans, and arrangements for lodging if the conference includes an overnight stay. The planning process involves all members of the patrol leaders' council and should accomplish the following tasks:

- Select the troop's program features for the coming year.
- Develop a program calendar that includes dates of troop activities, holidays, religious observances, school events, and dates important to the chartered organization.

PLC Annual Program Planning Conference Agenda

To help achieve the troop's goals, members of the patrol leaders' council can use the following outline for their annual program planning conference agenda.

1. **Develop troop goals for the coming year.**
    a. Advancement
    b. Community service
    c. Money earning

2. **Schedule major events.**
    a. Summer camp
    b. Scout shows
    c. Camporees
    d. Special troop events
    e. Good Turns
    f. Troop leadership training
    g. High-adventure activities

3. **Schedule special troop activities.**
    a. Boards of review
    b. Courts of honor
    c. Recruitment nights
    d. Webelos-to-Scout transition nights

4. **Select program features.**
    a. Select those of greatest interest to troop members.
    b. Determine their place in the troop calendar.
    c. Review their relevance to the troop's goals.
    d. Consider the advancement opportunities presented by each feature.

Once the program has been planned and the troop committee has added its support, copies of the plan should be distributed to troop members, their parents or guardians, and members of the troop committee.

To better understand the responsibility of the patrol leaders' council in annual program planning, see *The Scoutmaster Handbook.* Other important resources for all members of the patrol leaders' council are the program planning work sheets included in *Troop Program Features.*

Before the Annual Program Planning Conference

As a patrol leader, you will attend the annual program planning conference to be the spokesman for all the members of your patrol. Prior to the conference, you will meet with your patrol members to discuss the troop opportunities for the coming year that most appeal to them and to learn more about their personal goals and Scouting interests. Encourage patrol members to select and talk about the activities in the following list of program features that they find most inviting. The more information they give you about why and how the troop should accept their suggestions, the greater your ability to present their wishes during the planning conference.

Program Features

The BSA offers a wealth of exciting program features that can serve as a guide in planning a troop program. There are 36 program features offered in *Troop Program Features, Volumes I, II, and III.* Each program feature provides advancement opportunities, troop meeting outlines, and an outdoor event to top off the program feature.

Troop Program Features, Volume I, No. 33110	*Troop Program Features, Volume II,* No. 33111	*Troop Program Features, Volume III,* No. 33112

Program Features

Aquatics	Environment	Physical fitness
Athletics	First aid	Pioneering
Backpacking	Fishing	Public service
Boating/canoeing	Forestry	Safety
Business	Health care	Science
Camping	High adventure	Shooting
Citizenship	Hiking	Special cooking
Communications	Hobbies	Sports
Cooking	Leadership	Tracking
Cultural awareness	Mechanics	Wilderness survival
Emergency preparedness	Nature	Wildlife management
Engineering	Orienteering	Winter camping

Patrol Leaders' Council Monthly Meetings

The patrol leaders' council will meet every four weeks to put into action the program feature for the coming month. Schedule the monthly PLC meeting at the same time and place each month to make it easier for troop youth leaders to remember and fit the meeting into their schedules. The PLC can review the program feature and complete the plans for all of that month's troop meetings. The senior patrol leader will assign responsibility for specific portions of each troop meeting to particular patrols. Members of the PLC can discuss and finalize plans for the month's campouts or other troop activities and ensure that all members of the patrol leaders' conference understand the roles they are to play.

Prior to the meeting, the Scoutmaster may assist the senior patrol leader in developing a written agenda. The senior patrol leader should encourage members of the PLC to stick to the agenda so that all items of importance can be covered in a reasonable amount of time. A monthly meeting of the patrol leaders' council usually lasts no more than 90 minutes.

The Scoutmaster attends patrol leaders' council meetings as an observer and a resource. At the end of each meeting the Scoutmaster can close the proceedings with a general assessment of the meeting's important points, then offer positive reinforcement for all that went well.

Agenda for the Patrol Leaders' Council Monthly Meeting

The PLC monthly meeting should follow an agenda so that all items of business are covered. The following explains a sample agenda.

1. **Opening**
   The opening of a monthly PLC meeting could be a recitation of the Pledge of Allegiance or the Scout Oath and Law. It is an indication that it is time for council members to get down to business.

2. **Roll call and reading the log**
   The troop scribe records the attendance and then reads the log—that is, the minutes of the previous PLC meeting. Reading the log may not be necessary if everyone has had time to review the information before the meeting.

3. **Patrol reports**
   Each patrol leader is expected to come to the patrol leaders' council meeting prepared to give a brief report on the status of his patrol. The report can include announcements of advancement progress and information about any patrol activities that have occurred since the last meeting of the PLC.

4. **Old business**
   The senior patrol leader sets aside time for the council to discuss items mentioned in the minutes of the previous meeting that were unresolved or otherwise left undone. The group can determine what steps should be taken to close these matters.

5. **Planning the month's program features and big event**
   The troop's big event of the month (a campout, camporee, summer camp attendance, or other extended activity) requires careful planning. So does the program feature for the month to come. The patrol leaders' council should discuss these

portions of the troop's annual program, review the preparations that have occurred, and figure out what else must be done. The senior patrol leader can assign to various patrols the responsibilities for making final preparations.

6. **Planning the month's troop meetings**
    Each PLC member should have copies of the troop meeting plans for the coming month. With the help of the senior patrol leader, patrol leaders can finalize which patrol or troop leader will be accountable for each portion of the meetings. PLC members filling in the blank spots on their troop meeting plans can also include information about where to find the equipment and other items necessary for any of the month's games, skills instructions, or other meeting activities.

7. **New business**
    As the PLC meeting nears its conclusion, the senior patrol leader can bring up for discussion any new items of business and can invite PLC members to raise any issues they feel should be considered by the full council.

8. **Scoutmaster's Minute**
    The Scoutmaster will wrap up the meeting with a positive, motivational thought or story that will help pull the group together as a unified team.

Patrol Leaders' Council Meeting Agenda

Activity	Run by
Opening and Call to Order	Senior Patrol Leader
Roll Call and Reading of the Log (Minutes)	Troop Scribe
Patrol Reports	Patrol Leaders
Old Business	Senior Patrol Leader
Big Event Planning	Senior Patrol Leader
Troop Meeting Planning	Senior Patrol Leader
New Business	Senior Patrol Leader
Scoutmaster's Minute	Scoutmaster

Patrol Leaders' Council Stand-Up Meetings

A stand-up PLC meeting occurs in the minutes following the conclusion of every troop meeting. It is called "stand-up" because it is informal enough (and brief enough) to be conducted with members of the patrol leaders' council standing in a circle.

"In planning and carrying out the Scout program by patrols, your Scouts get valuable practice in group discussions and group decisions."

—"Green Bar" Bill Hillcourt

The point of the stand-up meeting is for the senior patrol leader to lead the rest of the PLC in a quick review and evaluation of the meeting that has just ended and to make sure that everyone is ready for the troop's next activity or meeting. The stand-up meeting can be used to suggest changes that need to be made in the troop's plan or to provide encouragement that certain Scouts or patrols need to make an extra effort to be ready for an event. The senior patrol leader can close the stand-up meeting with words of praise and positive reinforcement.

Leading
Patrol Meetings

Leading Patrol Meetings

A patrol meeting is an opportunity for you to lead
a group of Scouts as they conduct the business of the patrol. It
is also a chance for everyone in a patrol to learn new skills, plan
future activities, and have fun with friends.

Matters to be dealt with during a patrol meeting include taking
attendance, collecting dues, planning the patrol's involvement in
upcoming troop activities, selecting menus for hikes and campouts,
assigning patrol members to specific tasks, and working out any
other details for the smooth operation of the patrol. Depending on
how much business the patrols must handle, typical patrol meetings
can vary in length from five to 20 minutes or more.

When Patrols Meet

Patrol meetings may be held at any time and any place. The
patrol must consider the following when planning its meetings:

- A portion of most troop meetings will be set aside for each
  patrol to meet separately, often in the same room as the
  troop meeting.

- Patrols preparing for upcoming events may want to
  meet more frequently than patrols with lots of experience in a particular activity.

- A patrol may meet at the home of a patrol member on
  an evening other than that devoted to the troop meeting.

- Patrols can hold meetings during troop campouts and
  other outings, especially if there are unexpected develop-
  ments to address.

As a patrol leader, you will take charge of planning and running each patrol meeting. Plan what you want to accomplish at each meeting and think about how you will reach that goal. Whenever possible, delegate responsibility for portions of the meeting to other patrol members—someone to choose and lead an opening activity, for example, and someone else to prepare a closing.

Once a meeting begins, keep it on schedule by getting down to business. Eliminate sources of interruptions or distractions, and encourage patrol members to stay focused on the subjects of discussion. For example, if patrol members are unhappy about having to abandon an enjoyable game to start the meeting, you might let them know they can return to the game as soon as they have completed the work of being members of an active patrol.

Patrol meetings serve many different purposes. As a result, one meeting may differ greatly from the next. Whatever your intent, it's a good idea to begin each meeting by sharing with everyone the results you want to achieve by the time the meeting is done.

Planning the Meeting

You, the patrol leader, are in charge, but a patrol meeting should never become a one-man show. Every member of the patrol needs to be involved in some way. Whenever you can, make assignments in advance. That way patrol members will have time to get ready to present portions of the opening and closing of a meeting. They can also play an active role in the discussion of patrol business matters, the mastery of skills, and the setup of games.

The activities of a patrol usually follow the lead of the troop's annual program plan. A patrol that will take part in a troop hike, campout, or other big event can use meeting time to plan menus, develop equipment lists, and review essential skills that will allow members to make the most of the upcoming activity.

Now and then a patrol may wish to plan activities of its own—bicycling, hiking, visiting a museum, getting together to learn more about computers, or whatever else captures the patrol members' attention. As patrol leader, keep your ears open to hear what interests the members of your patrol. Ask them if they have suggestions for ways to build those interests into activities that can be enjoyed by everyone. During a patrol meeting you may want to engage members in some creative brainstorming, listing the patrol's ideas, and perhaps calling for a vote to determine where the greatest enthusiasm lies. That's democracy in action, an important principle of the patrol method.

The Patrol Meeting Agenda

A written agenda can help you plan a meeting and can guide you as the meeting unfolds. The agenda you prepare will include these key items:

1. **Opening**—This can be a call to order or a simple ceremony.
    - Scribe takes roll.
    - Scribe reads the log of the last meeting.
    - Patrol leader announces the purpose of the current meeting.
    - Assistant patrol leader reviews advancement by patrol members.

2. **Business**—Items of business may include one or more of the following:
    - Plan for upcoming activities and make assignments.
    - Address new business.
    - Present the patrol leader's report on the patrol leaders' council meeting (once a month).
    - Check and repair camping equipment.
    - Vote on issues that need to be decided.
    - Build patrol spirit (yell, song, flag, logo).

3. **Skill activity**—Practice a Scouting skill that will be needed in the future.

4. **Game**—Play a Scouting game. It may be selected from the troop's program resources.

5. **Closing**—Use a brief closing thought by the patrol leader or another member of the patrol to end the meeting and remind Scouts of the importance of what they are doing.

Patrol Meeting Plan

Date_____ Week _____

Activity	Description	Run By	Time
Opening _____ minutes			
Business _____ minutes			
Skill activity _____ minutes			
Game _____ minutes			
Closing _____ minutes			
After the Meeting			

Making Assignments

One of your early tasks will be to assign members to various positions of responsibility within the patrol. These may include assistant patrol leader, quartermaster, scribe, grubmaster, and cheermaster. If you have never made assignments before, your senior patrol leader and Scoutmaster can help you learn the process of coming up with good choices.

In addition to filling the patrol's official positions of responsibility, you can also determine what needs to be done to prepare for upcoming activities and then delegate portions of those preparations to members of the patrol—shopping for campout food, getting permission to use a certain area for an activity, or mending the patrol's tents and packing them for use, for example.

Drawing up a duty roster is a good way to figure out what needs to be done. By writing down who will take care of each task, you can make sure that every patrol member has a chance to share in the effort. Even new patrol members with little Scouting background can be penciled in to assist experienced Scouts in completing their assignments. Learning by doing under the watchful eye of an experienced Scout is an effective way for Scouts to master the basic skills of Scouting and to build the sense of belonging to their patrol.

Sample Duty Roster for a Week at Camp

	Stoves	Water	Cooking	Cleanup
Friday	Leo	Pham	Bob	Angelo
Saturday	Julio	Leo	Pham	Bob
Sunday	Frank	Julio	Leo	Pham
Monday	George	Frank	Julio	Leo
Tuesday	Angelo	George	Frank	Julio
Wednesday	Bob	Angelo	George	Frank
Thursday	Pham	Bob	Angelo	George

Checking Advancement Progress

Most Scouting activities present opportunities for a patrol member
to complete one or more requirements for rank advancement.
For example, going on a troop campout may fulfill a portion of
the camping requirement for a Scout earning the Second Class
rank. On the same campout he might complete another requirement by selecting the patrol's campsite and sleeping in a tent
he has pitched.

Patrol members can work together on certain assignments, too.
They may pool their resources and energies to plan and carry out
approved service projects that fulfill requirements for the ranks
of Star or Life. On other occasions, patrol members may unite to
participate in a flag ceremony for their school, religious institution,
chartered organization, community, or troop.

An important duty of the assistant patrol leader is to track the
advancement progress of each patrol member. Time can be set
aside at patrol meetings to review advancement progress and help
Scouts discover ways they can use patrol and troop activities to
complete rank requirements.

Scouting is a game with a purpose.

Fun is the game.
Values are the purpose.
Learning is the process.

Leading Patrol Activities

5

Leading Patrol Activities

The place where Scouting works best

is also where patrols most want to be—in the outdoors. Patrol members who spend time together outdoors share responsibilities, grow personally, and have plenty of fun-filled adventures. The outdoors is the best setting for Scouts to learn skills, to challenge themselves, and to practice respect of natural resources.

Why did you and the other members of the patrol join Scouting? Probably high on your list of reasons is the opportunity to hike and camp. As a patrol leader, you can help guide the patrol as its members plan and take part in terrific adventures in camp and on the trail.

Learning to Lead in the Outdoors

As a patrol leader you are experiencing hands-on training at its finest. You are learning leadership in the best possible way—by being a leader. Over time, you will discover that some meetings and activities that you lead go extremely well and everyone will recognize the patrol's success.

Of course, there will be times when plans fall through, when a meeting or an activity seems to be flat, or when there are unexpected challenges you must help the patrol confront. That's part of learning, too—doing the best you can with what you know at the moment, then figuring out how to do things better the next time around.

Camping

Every Scout troop strives to make camping a regular part of its program. During troop camping trips, the patrol usually will function
as a unit, establishing a campsite independent of other patrols but
not far from the rest of the troop. Patrol tents can be grouped
together, often with buddies sharing two-person tents. Your patrol
might also set up a dining fly to shelter the cooking area and provide a central gathering point. You will cook together as a patrol
and may take part as a group in other campout activities.

Your first campout as patrol leader is certain to present some
challenges. Planning and preparation are the keys to any patrol
activity. Do all you can to get ready for an adventure and you'll
be prepared to handle most situations. You will not be alone in
coming up with answers to questions you are sure to have. You
can always draw upon the ideas and strengths of other members
of the patrol and upon the experience of the troop's other leaders.

**One of the greatest
rewards for a patrol
leader is in helping
the members of the
patrol learn the
skills to camp well
and then in having
safe overnight
adventures sleep-
ing in tents or out
under the stars.**

Overnight Campouts

Troops try to plan at least one weekend campout each month. These campouts can be organized around hiking, backpacking, bicycling, canoeing, photography, nature study, or any of dozens of other Scouting skills. Whatever the focus of the weekend, members of each patrol plan their menus ahead of time, organize their gear, buy provisions for meals, and carry what they need to establish their camps.

Camporees

Now and then, a BSA council or district will host a camporee to bring together a number of troops for a weekend of camping fellowship. Camporees often have themes—orienteering or first aid, for example. Competitions can give your patrol a chance to show its stuff.

Camporees are fine opportunities for patrol members to get acquainted with Scouts from other troops and communities. The Scouts can practice many Scouting skills, too, and perhaps complete some rank requirements. As they share activities and campfires with others, they will be sharing in the excitement of building patrol spirit.

Summer Camps

A high point of the year for your troop can be spending a week at the local council's summer camp. As with other troop camping activities, you will camp as a patrol and take part in many camp activities together with other patrol members. Encourage everyone in your patrol to attend summer camp.

High-Adventure Treks

The Venture patrols of a troop may attend a high-adventure base operated by the BSA national office or by a BSA local council. These treks can involve extended backpacking expeditions, wilderness canoe trips, or boating on the open sea. In most cases they involve *moving camps*—that is, packing up each morning and hiking, paddling, rowing, floating, pedaling, or sailing to a different camp location.

High-adventure treks offer older Scouts a challenge that will test their skills and stamina. Patrols of younger Scouts can set their sights on high-adventure treks a year or two down the road, gaining valuable experience now with troop and patrol campouts, hikes, and other adventures closer to home. For more information on high-adventure treks, see *Passport to High Adventure.*

Hiking

Hiking can be one of a patrol's most rewarding adventures. A hike allows patrol members to be together in new surroundings, to function as a group, and to have a fine time. While hiking, patrol members can gain the confidence and skills that will prepare them for campouts and other longer-term activities.

Hikes are often very simple. Members of the patrol can decide on a destination and then allow the adventure to develop while walking. By remembering to keep their eyes and ears open, patrol members are likely to see and hear much that will capture their interest.

I'm Happy When I'm Hiking

English hiking song

Tramp, tramp, tramp, tramp, tramp, tramp, tramp, tramp.

I'm hap - py when I'm hik - ing, pack up - on my back. I'm hap - py when I'm hik - ing off the beat - en track. Out in the o - pen coun - try, that's the place for me. With a true Scout-ing friend to the jour-ney's end, ten, twen-ty, thir - ty, for - ty, fif - ty miles a day. Tramp, tramp, tramp. *(Repeat tramp to end.)*

Copyright by Neil A. Kjos Music Co., Chicago. Used by permission.

Other hikes can be structured to achieve certain goals. An orienteering hike, for example, will provide patrol members with good reason to use maps and compasses to find their way. Nature hikes can fix their attention on wildlife and vegetation, and they can be especially successful if the patrol is accompanied by someone with a knowledge of local plants and animals. On another well-planned hike, patrol members who have been practicing first aid might come across a staged accident scene where they can use their new knowledge to deal with a realistic "emergency."

Hiking adventures are limited only by the imaginations of patrol members. Here are some possibilities for adventurous hikes.

Orienteering Hikes

When the patrol has mastered the basics of using a map and compass, you can chart a route on a topography map and then follow it to a destination. Before setting out, determine five or six landmarks along the way—hilltops, lakes, buildings, and so on. These will serve as indicators that you are staying on course. Patrol members can travel as a group on some orienteering hikes, putting their heads together to figure out which way to go. During other outings, divide the patrol into teams of two or three Scouts. Teams can set out along the route at five-minute intervals, each with a compass and a map.

A High-Tech Hike

Does your patrol have access to a handheld receiver for a global positioning system (GPS)? Ask your senior patrol leader or an assistant Scoutmaster to help you by stashing a reward (a bag of hard candies, for example) at a secret location, then use the GPS receiver to record  the exact route from a trailhead to that spot. Scouts setting out later on the high-tech hike can use the same receiver to backtrack along the original route. If their readings are correct, they will come upon their reward.

Exploration Hikes

Hikes into territory that is new to all members of the patrol can be especially satisfying. Perhaps there is a mountain, a forest, or an ocean shore to explore. Your patrol might go off in search of the source of a small stream or to observe deer grazing in a meadow. An exploration hike may take your patrol cross-country or along back roads and trails. Whatever the route, it is sure to be full of surprises.

Nature Hikes

Patrol members can discuss and choose the sort of nature hike they would like to experience—tree identification, wildlife viewing, star study, or examining creatures in lakes, ponds, or tidal pools, for example. Troop leaders may be able to suggest a merit badge counselor or other expert in the selected subject who can go along to help the patrol members enjoy the hike to its fullest.

Tracking Hikes

Footprints and other signs left by wild animals tell fascinating stories about their activities. Patrol members may wish to photograph tracks or make plaster casts of them. While animal signs can be found in many terrains and conditions, they are easiest to observe in snow and in the moist soil along streams and lakes.

Parent-Son Hikes

Patrol members can plan a hike that includes parents or guardians. Along the way, such a hike can include a picnic lunch and lots of shared enjoyment as Scouts teach the adults a few Scouting skills. The hike might end with an evening campfire program featuring skits and songs offered both by Scouts and adults.

The degree of difficulty of any hike should match the experience and maturity level of the patrol members. The first hikes undertaken by a patrol ought to be relatively easy. As patrol members develop greater skill, the hikes they enjoy can become increasingly lengthy and challenging.

Patrol Leader Hike Responsibilities

Emphasize safety on every Scout outing. Encourage patrol members to dress for expected weather conditions and to wear shoes or boots that are comfortable and sturdy. Warn them to be on guard against hypothermia during chilly or wet weather. Patrol leaders should be prepared to implement a plan of action in case of emergency. Another important responsibility during a hike is to keep the patrol members together. A good way to do this is to encourage every Scout to hike with a buddy.

Plan patrol hike routes that avoid roads or that keep to quiet back roads with little traffic. When road walking cannot be avoided, stay on the left side of the roadway facing oncoming traffic. Keep night hiking along roads to a minimum, and continue in the dark only if Scouts make themselves visible by carrying flashlights and by wearing light-colored clothing, reflective vests, or white cloths tied around their right legs. Never allow hitchhiking—it may be dangerous, and it spoils the spirit of a Scout adventure.

Leave No Trace

All members of the Boy Scouts of America protect the environment by following the principles of Leave No Trace whenever they are in outdoor settings. The Leave No Trace principles are fully discussed in the *Boy Scout Handbook, Fieldbook,* and the publications and Web sites of Leave No Trace Inc.

Principles of Leave No Trace

 Plan ahead and prepare.

 Travel and camp on durable surfaces.

 Dispose of waste properly. (Pack it in, pack it out.)

 Leave what you find.

 Respect wildlife.

 Minimize campfire impacts.

 Be considerate of other visitors.

In addition to following the principles of Leave No Trace, Scouting's commitment to wise conservation practices is expressed in the BSA's Outdoor Code.

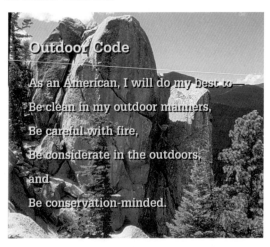

Outdoor Code

As an American, I will do my best to—

Be clean in my outdoor manners,

Be careful with fire,

Be considerate in the outdoors, and

Be conservation-minded.

Patrol Trip Plan

Once the Scoutmaster approves the general plan for a patrol hike, troop campout, patrol overnight, or other Scouting activity, your patrol will get together to answer the five W's of the upcoming adventure—where, when, who, why and what—and one question about Leave No Trace. Discussing these questions will give the patrol members the guidance they need to get themselves ready.

- **Where are we going?** Decide on the destination and the route you plan to take. Where is the starting point and ending point of the trek? In some cases it will be appropriate to provide adult Scout leaders and parents with copies of a map marked with the intended route.

- **When will we return?** If the patrol has not returned within a couple of hours of the time estimated on its trip plan, Scout leaders can take appropriate action.

- **Who is going with us?** List names of each patrol member who is going on the hike.

- **Why are we going?** What is purpose of the hike? The answer to this question will help the patrol take what it needs and make the most of the opportunities that present themselves.

- **What are we taking?** For most Scout outings, the outdoor essentials form the core of the items every patrol member should carry. Longer trips, cold-weather journeys, and adventures involving camping out will require additional gear, clothing, and food for each Scout and for the patrol as a group.

- **How will we follow the principles of Leave No Trace?** Review the Leave No Trace principles and think about the ways patrol members can stick to each one of them. Once in the field, keep the principles in mind and use them as reminders of the best ways to enjoy the outdoors.

Patrol Trip Plan

Trip plan of _____

Where:
Destination _____
Route going _____
_____

Route returning_____
_____

When:
Date and time of departure _____
Date and time of return _____

Who:
Names of persons taking part _____
_____

Why:
Purpose of the trip_____
_____

What:
☑ Gear and other items to be taken:
☐ Outdoor essentials
☐ Other clothing and gear_____
_____
Permits required_____
Special equipment needs _____
Special clothing needs _____

How:
List the principles of Leave No Trace that relate to your trip. For each one, write a sentence explaining what the patrol will do to follow that principle. _____
_____
_____
_____

The Outdoor Essentials

Patrol members who carry the outdoor essentials during Scout activities in the outdoors will be prepared to handle most situations they encounter. By planning ahead, they can add additional items of clothing, gear, and food in anticipation of more demanding challenges.

- ☑ The outdoor essentials
- ☐ Pocketknife
- ☐ First-aid kit
- ☐ Extra clothing
- ☐ Rain gear
- ☐ Water bottle
- ☐ Flashlight
- ☐ Trail food
- ☐ Matches and fire starters
- ☐ Sun protection
- ☐ Map and compass

For more on the outdoor essentials, and for lists of clothing and gear for outdoor patrol activities, see *The Boy Scout Handbook* and *Fieldbook.*

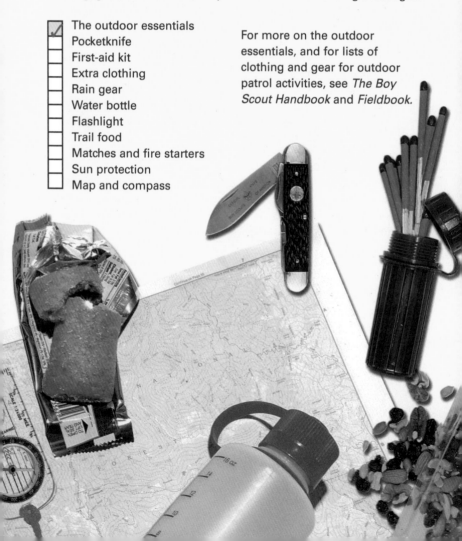

Other Patrol Activities

Not all patrol activities take place in the outdoors. The patrol may be called upon to perform several duties in service to the troop or the community.

Ceremonies

The patrol often will be invited to take part in ceremonies at troop meetings, camporees, and other Scouting events. It may have responsibility for a flag ceremony at the beginning of a meeting, a recitation of the Scout Oath and Law at a campfire, or a presentation at a court of honor, parents' night, or other public event.

A good ceremony does not happen by accident. When your patrol is asked to conduct a ceremony, plan it well and then rehearse the various roles. Keep it simple and be sure each patrol member understands what he is to do.

Patrol Service Projects

Members of the Boy Scouts of America historically have provided service to others. Scout service projects benefit communities, organizations, individuals, and the environment while building character and good citizenship among Scouts involved in those efforts.

Service projects are most often done by troops, but now and then a patrol may want to undertake a special project on its own. After receiving approval from the patrol leaders' council, members of the patrol can begin planning the project. Keep the Scoutmaster and the patrol leaders' council fully informed about the project and the progress the patrol is making.

"I like to think that faithful observance of the Scout Oath constitutes an excellent preliminary training in the duties of citizenship. I like to think of the entire Scout training as an apprenticeship for the mastery of future civil duties."

—*Franklin D. Roosevelt, 32nd president of the United States, 1933-1945*

Campfires

A Scout's fondest memories often are created in front of a patrol campfire. The warmth and glow of the embers and the time together with patrol members can encourage fellowship and reflection. Of course, the experience of a patrol campfire doesn't require an actual fire; patrol members enjoying the view from a quiet riverbank or hillside can discover every bit as much meaning and friendship. Where campfires are not appropriate, a lantern or candle can serve as the centerpiece of a patrol's evening.

With or without a fire, patrol gatherings should be fun. They can include skits, lively songs, storytelling, and the observance of the natural setting of the camp. For more on developing campfire programs that begin lively and end with quiet, inspiring thoughts, see the BSA's Campfire Program Planner.

Games

Games can be effective team-building activities for the patrol.
Those that rely on the cooperative efforts of all patrol members
for success can be especially effective on building patrol spirit.

Keep these pointers in mind as you and the members of your
patrol are planning games:

- Seek variety. Don't play the same game over and over.

- Include everyone.

- Keep track of time. Bring a game to a close while everyone is
  still having a good time.

- Choose simple games that require few rules and little equipment.

- Weather permitting, play the game outdoors.

For more on games that require patrol teamwork and
cooperation, see the initiative game section of the BSA's *Troop
Program Resources*.

Songs

A lively song on the trail can help pass the miles and can do wonders for patrol spirit. Songs are part of campfires and may be included in troop meetings, courts of honor, and other Scout gatherings. Some members of the patrol may love to sing, while others can be shy about it. Whatever the case, encourage the patrol to make singing a regular part of its activities. You may wish to select a patrol song leader who can lead the patrol in learning and enjoying new songs. The *Boy Scout Songbook* is a good resource for song ideas.

Worship

Scouting can bring patrol members together with the natural world in ways that are inspirational and spiritual. As you plan patrol and troop activities, the troop chaplain can help determine ways for patrol members to fulfill their religious obligations and to respect the beliefs of others.

Saying Grace

The grace offered at the beginning of a meal can be led by a patrol member. Examples of blessings include:

- *Bless us, O Lord, and these Thy gifts which we are about to receive from Thy bounty, through Christ, our Lord, Amen.*—Catholic
- *Gracious Giver of all good,*
  Thee we thank for rest and food.
  Grant that all we do or say,
  In Thy service be this day. Amen.—Protestant
- *Blessed art You O Lord our God, Ruler of the universe, Who brings forth bread from the earth.*—Jewish
- *For food, for raiment, for life, for opportunity—for friendship and fellowship—we thank Thee, O Lord.*—Philmont Scout Ranch Grace

6 Being a Good Leader

THE SIX SHOOTERS

TROOP
603

GOLDEN EMPIRE
COUNCIL

CHAPTER SIX

Being a Good Leader

Think of some of the best leaders

you have known. Perhaps there is a teacher at your school who seems gifted with the ability to guide people toward their goals. Maybe you are on a team coached by someone who inspires you to achieve the most that you can. You might have noticed the skill with which your Scoutmaster and senior patrol leader move the troop along.

Now that you have become the leader of a patrol, you may be asking yourself how you can be most effective in your new role. What steps can you take to lead well?

Basics of Leadership

There are almost as many methods of leadership as there are leaders. All good leaders develop their own styles, building on their successes and learning from experiences that were not so positive. Approaches to leadership that are effective for one person may not work at all for someone else. Leaders may also discover that the methods they use will change depending on the people they are leading and the challenges their groups are facing.

Even so, there are some basics of leadership that can give you a head start in developing your own approach to being a patrol leader. Among the most important are these:

❶ Have a good attitude.

❷ Act with maturity.

❸ Be organized.

❹ Look the part.

Have a Good Attitude

An optimistic outlook is infectious. Maintain a positive, can-do attitude, and those around you will find that they share your enthusiasm. You don't have to be noisy about it; simply be willing to do your best all the time. Instead of feeling defeated by the challenges facing the patrol, set about the business of using the combined strengths of all patrol members to find good solutions.

"What you do your-selves, your Scouts will do also."

—*Robert Baden-Powell*

Act With Maturity

Earn the respect of those you are leading by being fair to everyone and consistent in your actions. It is important to be flexible enough to change direction when that will be best for the patrol, but there is nothing more confusing than a leader who flip-flops on his decisions without clear reason. Likewise, a patrol leader who treats some Scouts more favorably than others will soon lose the group's trust. Patrol members will respond well to your leadership when they know what to expect from you.

Be Organized

Careful preparations before meetings and patrol events will pay off many times over in the success of those activities. Patrol members will receive the message that you care enough about them to put energy into planning the best possible experiences for the entire patrol.

Look the Part

Leadership comes from within, not from the shirt on your back or the patch on your shoulder. On the other hand, the Boy Scout uniform does command respect. It provides identity for troop members. It can strengthen the sense of belonging and build patrol spirit.

Set a good example for the patrol by wearing the full Boy Scout uniform whenever it is appropriate. Follow these guidelines:

- Patrol leaders and patrol members proudly wear the full uniform for all ceremonial activities, including boards of review, courts of honor, patriotic events, parades, and special occasions at troop meetings and summer camp.

- During physically active outdoor events and informal patrol and troop meetings, patrol members may wear the BSA activity uniform—troop or camp T-shirts with Scout pants or shorts.

- Scouts participating in patrol and troop conservation projects, other service work, or backcountry camping may wear work pants or jeans with their troop or camp T-shirts.

Key Leadership Skills

In addition to the basics of leadership, several other skills will allow you to guide the patrol well. Four of these are:

❶ Effective communication

❷ Effective listening

❸ Start, Stop, Continue

❹ Matching leadership style to leadership needs

Effective Communication

Communicating effectively is more than just visiting with someone, especially when you are giving and receiving important information. At a patrol meeting or during a patrol activity, you will sometimes be challenged to explain detailed information to other patrol members so that all of them clearly understand. Here are some methods that may allow you to communicate better with the patrol.

GIVING INFORMATION

Assume you have just attended a patrol leaders' council meeting to plan an upcoming troop campout. Now you need to share the information with members of the patrol.

- Before you begin, take a moment to organize your thoughts. You may want to write a few notes to remind yourself of the points you want to cover.

- Have the patrol members gather in a place free of distractions. If you are outdoors on a bright day, turn so that you, rather than the listeners, are facing the sun. Don't begin until you have everyone's attention. You can hold up the Scout sign as a signal that it is time for everyone to focus on the business at hand.

- Speak clearly. Make eye contact with listeners. As you finish explaining each item, ask if there are any questions.

- If possible, write the most important points on a flip chart or chalkboard.

- Repeat facts such as dates, times, and places.

- Ask the patrol scribe to make notes of the discussion. He can also distribute copies of schedules, activity plans, or duty rosters to members of the patrol.

RECEIVING INFORMATION

Communication is a two-way street. When you are in a position to receive information, give it your full attention. Create an atmosphere for communication by doing the following:

- Give the speaker your full attention.

- Write down points of information—dates, times, locations, etc.

- If you are unclear about anything, ask questions.

Effective Listening

As you can see from the discussion of giving and receiving information, effective listening is essential to good communication. Effective listening is also a skill that each of us can learn and can constantly improve.

Most of us love to hear the sounds of our own voices. In conversations, we may think more about what we are going to say next than about what is being said by others. When you are in conversations with members of your patrol, though, practice good listening by paying close attention to what others are saying and also to what they are leaving unsaid. Notice their tone of voice and watch their body language. Try to listen without passing judgment.

❶ **Effective listening is vital for forming relationships, finding solutions, and developing patrol spirit.**

Be aware, too, of how you are feeling while you listen. Are you chilly, hungry, sleepy, too hot, too cold, or late for another meeting? Is the speaker's message something you don't want to hear? Any of these factors can have an impact on your attention span. If you are upset, angry, or worried, that can affect your ability to listen well.

❷ **Effective listening can be a tool for turning a negative situation into a positive one.**

Noticing how you feel can help you better grasp what others are saying. The adjustment you make might simply be a matter of focusing more on a speaker's message. Often, though, it may require calling a time-out so that you can put on a sweater, have a bite to eat, take care of distracting matters, or let your emotions cool down. When you get back together with the speaker, the conditions may be much more inviting to good listening.

Of course, you cannot tailor every listening situation. Now and then you will find yourself in discussions with others when communications are difficult. Continually practice effective listening, though, and you will find that it can be a powerful tool for solving problems, settling disputes, and building patrol spirit.

FOLLOW-UP

Communicating well is a constant goal of a patrol leader. It is your responsibility to keep patrol members aware of activities for the patrol and troop. But sometimes when a patrol member is absent from a patrol meeting, he won't get important information along with other patrol members. Sometimes plans you have discussed with the patrol members must be changed, perhaps at the last minute.

The follow-up steps you take in these situations can ensure that effective communication continues:

- Make a list of the phone numbers and e-mail addresses of the members of your patrol. Use it to contact everyone if you need to relay information outside of a scheduled meeting.

- Give patrol members as much advance notice as possible concerning upcoming activities. If you wait until the last minute, some patrol members may have scheduling conflicts.

- Whenever possible, provide patrol members with written copies of important information—duty rosters, calendars of events, etc.

- Remind patrol members of specific duties they have accepted, such as buying the food for a campout.

- Maintain a patrol calendar for keeping track of upcoming patrol and troop activities.

- Discuss patrol activities with your parents or guardian. They need to know your schedule and may be an important resource for ideas and support.

- Plan, plan, plan. Fill out a planning work sheet on every activity.

Start, Stop, Continue

Start, Stop, Continue is a series of questions designed to help troop members assess an event or activity that has just occurred and explore some of the values that activity offers. The troop can then take the outcome and focus on reapplication and future events. Troops that use SSC are less likely to end up with an emphasis on what went wrong than when using other assessment tools. In its simplest form, SSC is three questions:

1. What should we *start* doing that would make us more successful?

2. What should we *stop* doing that is not working or is a barrier to our success?

3. What should we *continue* to do because it was a significant reason for our success?

For major events and when you are a more experienced leader, the group can explore the *why* of each question. The answers often will help to reinforce the values of the Scout Oath and Law in the experience.

Some key points for using the SSC assessment tool:

- Everyone has the right to express his thoughts.

- Each person has the choice of talking or remaining silent.

- No one may interrupt the person speaking, and there is no room for put-downs or making fun of someone.

- Gathering input here is key, but it is not always necessary to evaluate and reach consensus. The patrol leaders' council may be the right place to review the input and apply a solution.

- Do not allow the discussion to become negative or focus on individuals.

To end the discussion, summarize the most important points that were mentioned. When appropriate, the troop scribe should keep a record to be shared at the next patrol leaders' council meeting. Be positive throughout the session and as you bring it to a close.

Matching Leadership Styles to Leadership Needs

Effective leaders nearly always have more than one leadership style. A key to good leadership is to match the style of leadership to the situation. For instance, a First Class Scout who has been in the troop for a year or more may require little or no guidance on a weekend camping trip, but a new Scout on his first camp-out will probably need lots of attention, encouragement, and instruction.

Among the most common styles of leadership are:

• Explaining

• Demonstrating

• Guiding

• Enabling

THE EXPLAINING STYLE

Explaining is a leadership style used when patrol members are just beginning in a task or skill. They are enthusiastic but really do not have the skill or knowledge to do what needs to be done. When a patrol or an individual is at this stage, the leaders need to carefully *explain* what must be done, how to do it, and what the result needs to be.

THE DEMONSTRATING STYLE

When the patrol or an individual is just learning a new skill, frustration can come quickly when the skill just isn't there yet. The leader at this point needs to use the *demonstrating* style of leadership, showing precisely how something is to be done. He also must model the behavior expected of patrol members.

THE GUIDING STYLE

As the patrol or members get better at a task or skill, they will exhibit a growing enthusiasm and motivation. The leader's response to this should be to step back and give them plenty of room to act on their own, but be ready to coach and *guide* when help is needed. An example might be the patrol leader performing his responsibilities during meal preparation but remaining close by and ready to help others, if they need it. That will help *guide* them toward being successful.

THE ENABLING STYLE

Enabling is leadership style that can be used when skills are high to create an environment of continued success. It means the leader can delegate teaching responsibility for that task or skill to the individual or patrol. The leader recognizes that the group has reached proficiency, and he can and should express his confidence in them.

Helping the Patrol Develop as a Team

Understanding how patrols develop can help you better match your leadership style to the needs of all patrol members. In turn, that can encourage everyone to move forward, which helps a troop to achieve as much as it can.

Theories of Team Development

There are many theories explaining how teams like patrols and troops evolve. At the council-level National Youth Leadership Training, you will learn that teams go through a progression of stages, each requiring a different leadership approach. The Leading EDGE (Explain, Demonstrate, Guide, Enable) is the same term used to describe a process for teaching a skill, but here it describes the series of leadership behaviors you just learned.

Just as you can adjust your leadership styles to match the needs of individuals, you can address the needs of an entire patrol, too. The key is this: Figure out what the patrol is missing and then provide it.

Supporting the Patrol

To discover what the patrol requires from you, pay attention. Watch patrol members as they interact with one another. Listen to their comments and concerns and think about ways you can help each of them reach their full potential.

For example, members of a newly formed patrol usually are eager to fit in. They may be unsure about what is expected of them, though, and will need lots of guidance. Take time to establish personal connections with each Scout and learn about his interests and talents. The *explaining style* and the *demonstrating style* you use with individuals can also be used with great effect in group leadership situations when applied to a newly formed patrol.

Patrol members who have been around for a while should have developed quite a bit of skill in resolving their difficulties and achieving many of the goals they have set for themselves. They should be confident in their ability to perform tasks and to overcome obstacles. They have a sense of pride in belonging to a successful patrol, and they enjoy working together. The trust and respect they have for one another is high.

You can support experienced patrols by seeing to it that members have everything they require to continue succeeding. Those resources may be in the form of materials, camping gear, or knowledge, especially information you can share from meetings of the patrol leaders' council. Recognize individuals for their accomplishments, too, and encourage open communication. You may find that the *guiding style* and *enabling style* of leadership are just right for bringing out the best in a veteran patrol.

Providing Leadership to the Patrol

- Rely on shared values as you make ethical choices in patrol leadership. The Scout Law and Oath are expressions of the BSA's values, and shared values are a foundation of any team.

- Offer a vision of success. The troop's annual program plan is a blueprint for exciting activities and outdoor adventures. Use it to focus the patrol members' energy and enthusiasm.

- Recognize that some patrol members may be advancing faster than others. Give additional assistance to Scouts taking additional time to learn skills and to gain Scouting experience. Offer advanced Scouts added responsibilities and leadership positions, and allow them to help others.

- Model the kind of behavior and achievement you expect from everyone in the patrol. Be what you want them to be. Have high expectations for yourself, and expect the best in others.

- Acknowledge differences. Look for ways to draw on individual strengths of Scouts to the advantage of the entire patrol. Develop trust by keeping the interests of patrol members in mind.

- Make meetings count. Get down to the business of making things happen and of having fun along the way.

- Respect and value others. Help each Scout feel that he has something important to contribute to the success of the patrol.

Overcoming Patrol Disappointments

Now and then a patrol may become discouraged. Perhaps Scouts are discovering the reality of the challenges facing them. A campout or other planned activity that didn't go very well may cause some Scouts to become frustrated.

You will be tested as a patrol leader when the spirits of patrol members are down. Draw upon your abilities to communicate clearly, listen actively, and encourage open discussions. Recognize patrol accomplishments and offer encouragement and reassurance to those Scouts who are making efforts to achieve. Start, Stop, Continue can be an effective tool for helping you discover what is at the root of patrol members' discontent and for helping Scouts find their own solutions to the situation.

Celebrating Success

Now and then patrol members will achieve significant milestones together or even complete their time together as a tight-knit group. Some patrol members may be moving on to form a Venture crew, for example. Members of a new-Scout patrol may have reached a level of experience and advancement to be ready to join the regular patrols of the troop.

> "It is up to the patrol leader to take hold of and develop the qualities of each boy in his patrol. It sounds like a big order, but in practice it works."
>
> —*Robert Baden-Powell*

Whatever the case, celebrate the many accomplishments that patrol members have enjoyed during their time together. Documenting the patrol's history with a scrapbook or photo album can be an enjoyable way to create a record of all that the Scouts have accomplished.

Putting Out Fires

Being a patrol leader is not always an easy task, nor is it always a popular position. There may even be times when you want to give your patrol leader's patch back to the Scoutmaster. But if leadership were always easy, everyone would do it. It's when the challenges of leadership become difficult—when you need to put out fires—that you will know you will gain some of the most valuable experience in becoming a good leader.

Difficult leadership situations come in many forms. A patrol member may not be aware that his behavior was out of line or may not understand that what he is doing compromises the safety of other Scouts. A patrol member having problems at home or in school may let out his anger during a patrol activity. Sometimes a Scout may simply want to challenge your leadership.

When a personality issue surfaces, others in your patrol will be watching to see how you handle things. They will sense if you are being fair and if you are seeking workable solutions. In short, they will be watching to see if you really are a leader.

A few guidelines can serve you well as you cope with difficult leadership issues:

- Remain as calm as you can. Don't get mad. Stay focused on finding a solution.

- If possible, meet privately with those who are upset. That will give everyone a chance to air concerns without an audience.

- Use open-ended questions to explore differences:

  —If you were patrol leader, what would you do?

  —How can we solve the problem as a patrol?

  —What are you willing to do to resolve this situation?

- Be firm and state the case clearly, especially if the problem involves safety issues or Scouting policies with nonnegotiable guidelines.

Consider these effective responses to Scouts whose behavior requires some action from the patrol leader:

- "Mark, it looked like you were giving that new Scout a hard time. I'm sure you know that's not an acceptable way to treat others. Tell me what's going on and let's talk about some ways we older Scouts can help these new guys."

- "Jim, our patrol is a team, and each patrol member has a task to do. Let's consider some ways you can take more responsibility for doing your share."

- "Bob, you seem to be second-guessing me on everything. Let's talk about why that is happening and how we can work out a better way of dealing with each other."

The other person may be argumentative, even hostile. Stay calm, letting him know that you are hearing what he is saying. A simple "I got it" is a good response. Keep the dialogue going with open comments:

- "I hear what you are saying. Let's look at that another way."

- "I hear what you are saying. How can we change what you are doing so it is within the Scouting guidelines?"

- "I hear what you are saying. Let's look for some ways that this will work for everyone in the patrol."

Serious problems such as those involving drugs, alcohol, hazing, or harassment should be reported to troop leadership immediately.

Sample Leadership Problem-Solving Situations

Here are five situations you may encounter as a patrol leader, each followed by one of the many appropriate solutions. Read each situation and consider how you would handle the problem.

ON THE TRAIL

Your patrol is on a 10-mile hike to a destination that is new to everyone. An assistant Scoutmaster is leading the hike and the Scoutmaster is hiking at the back of the troop. You notice that the assistant Scoutmaster and several Scouts are hiking so quickly they have disappeared up the trail. You mention this to the Scoutmaster, who asks you to handle the situation.

> **One solution:** You and another patrol member jog up the trail to catch the others. When you catch them, you ask to speak to the assistant Scoutmaster. Moving off the trail out of the hearing of the other Scouts, you share your concern they should stay with the rest of the troop and suggest that the new-Scout patrol join the assistant Scoutmaster at the head of the troop where they can set the pace.

AT A TROOP FEAST

The troop is planning a feast. At the patrol leaders' council meeting your patrol was assigned to select and prepare the main course. The members of your patrol want to prepare spaghetti and meatballs, but you are a vegetarian and never eat meat. What can you do?

> **One solution:** You were elected to be the representative of your patrol and should do your best to allow the patrol members to achieve all they can within the plans of the patrol leaders' council. As a member of the patrol, your interests are also important. You lead the patrol in a discussion to find a solution that works for every patrol member, including you. In this case, it may involve preparing two dishes of spaghetti sauce, one with meatballs and one without.

AT SCOUT CAMP

On the second day of summer camp, the assistant patrol leader tells you that a Scout in your patrol is not taking part in archery because a boy from another troop has been picking on him. What do you do?

One solution: Speak with the Scout away from the hearing of others, and ask him if there are any problems with his camping experience that he would like to talk about. Encourage him to tell his side of the story of what happened at the archery range. Listen closely to his answer and consider his attitude. Did the assistant patrol leader seem to get it right? Does the Scout see things differently?

Once you understand the situation, work with the Scout to come up with a good solution. It may be that he needs nothing more than to know his patrol supports him. There could be a different archery session the Scout could attend. It might be appropriate to talk with the boy who is picking on the Scout or to have a word with the archery instructor. Encourage your patrol member to help you figure out an answer to the problem so that he can return to the archery range and get the most out of his Scouting experience.

AT A TROOP MEETING

The senior patrol leader telephones you at home to let you know several Webelos Scouts will be visiting the troop meeting the following night. He would like your patrol to take responsibility for presenting an impressive opening flag ceremony. The entire patrol will need to arrive at the troop meeting place early and in full uniform. What do you do?

One solution: Telephone all the members of your patrol and pass the word on to each of them.

BACKPACKING

At the last meeting, patrol members divided up the patrol tents, cooking gear, and other group equipment for a weekend backpacking trip, assigning heavier items to the bigger, stronger hikers and lighter gear to smaller Scouts. Saturday morning at the trailhead, though, one member of your patrol refuses to carry his share. What do you do?

One solution: Talk to the Scout out of the hearing of others. First, try to determine why the Scout is reluctant to carry his load. Perhaps his pack is out of adjustment and uncomfortable, or he is afraid he will tire quickly and become embarrassed in front of the rest of the patrol. He may have brought too much personal gear that is weighing down his pack.

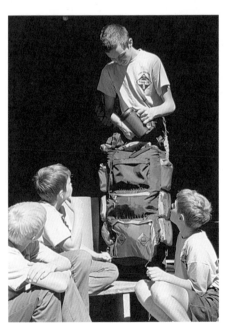

Try to find a solution together—fixing his pack, leaving behind some unnecessary personal items, or reminding him that you and the patrol will support him even if he is not the strongest hiker in the group. If there seems to be no clear cause for his concern, remind him that a patrol is a democracy in which every member has an equal voice and equal responsibilities. By doing his part, he makes it possible for the entire patrol to succeed.

Conflict Resolution

Conflicts can occur when people disagreeing with each other seem unable to find a reasonable compromise. The roots of these disagreements can arise from many sources, including differences in personality, values, and perceptions.

As a patrol leader, you will need to handle the differences that arise among members of the patrol. Those conflicts may be minor, or they may fester into something that can damage patrol spirit and the ability of the patrol members to work together effectively.

Responses to Conflict

Your response to a perceived conflict probably will take one of three forms:

❶ Avoiding

❷ Compromising

❸ Problem solving

AVOIDING

Avoiding a problem seldom makes it go away, but there are times when it is best to let others work out their differences on their own. By using the skills of effective listening, you should have a good feel for the quality of the relationships among patrol members and should be able to decide when to help resolve a disagreement.

An important time for you to step in is when the patrol members themselves are avoiding a problem by shying away from the steps that would lead to a resolution of a disagreement. They may have decided simply not to talk about it, but without communication, there can be no progress.

COMPROMISING

In solving a conflict by compromise, both parties must be willing to give up something to gain something more. Reaching that point may require the assistance of a negotiator—in this case, you, the patrol leader.

PROBLEM SOLVING

The most effective way to resolve conflicts is for all parties to explain their points of view and to become convinced that they should exert effort to solve the problem. As in compromising, a negotiator may serve as a guide to help them resolve their differences.

The Patrol Leader as Conflict Negotiator

When two members of your patrol are in disagreement, you can often find a workable solution by using many of the same skills that are effective when the actions of a single person are unacceptable. Stay calm. Use open-ended questions to get each patrol member to explain his understanding of the problem. Encourage each patrol member to see the situation from the other's point of view, then enlist their aid in working together to find a solution that is agreeable to everyone.

Dealing With Inappropriate Behavior

The Scouting program offers young people opportunities to learn and grow in a setting where they can enjoy the acceptance and support of others. Hazing, harassment, name-calling, and bullying have no place in Scouting and will not be tolerated. Likewise, cheating, stealing, lying, cursing, vandalism, fighting, and other forms of inappropriate behavior must be firmly addressed by a Scout troop.

Scouting is built upon the youth-led troop and youth-led patrol. As a patrol leader, you set an example for the behavior of everyone in the patrol. When you see that a patrol member is overstepping the boundaries of the code of conduct spelled out in the Scout Oath and Law, it is your responsibility to step aside with that Scout and discuss with him why his behavior is not acceptable.

Serious or recurring inappropriate behavior should be reported to the Scoutmaster and senior patrol leader. The patrol leaders' council may become involved in discussing certain behavioral problems. Disruptive behavior on the part of an individual Scout may be referred to the Scoutmaster and troop committee, who will, in turn, involve the Scout's parents or guardian in a cooperative effort to resolve the issue.

"The thing is to cooperate happily in the process which develops discipline and obedience in the doing of small things while we are young. Then, when our turn comes to do big things, discipline will help to ensure accomplishment."

—James E. West, the BSA's first Chief Scout Executive

7 Other Patrol Leadership Positions

Other Patrol Leadership Positions

One of the most satisfying aspects

of leading a patrol is sharing that leadership. Give every patrol member a specific responsibility, make sure he understands the task, provide him with the guidance and resources he needs, and you soon will discover that your patrol is exciting, active, and lively.

As a patrol leader, you will have the opportunity to match the right patrol member with the right position. You will appoint a Scout to serve as assistant patrol leader. Other positions that may be filled by members of the patrol are patrol scribe, patrol quartermaster, patrol grubmaster, and patrol cheermaster.

Assistant Patrol Leader

The assistant patrol leader takes charge of the patrol whenever you are not available. He should be a strong ally for you, someone who can be relied upon to help the patrol move forward. You will keep him fully informed about what is going on with the patrol and can use him as a sounding board when you must make tough decisions.

The duties of the assistant patrol leader include:

- Assist the patrol leader in planning and chairing patrol meetings.

- Lend a hand in leading patrol activities and building patrol spirit.

- Help the patrol prepare for troop activities.

- Assist the scribe in keeping current the advancement records of patrol members.

- Monitor the advancement progress of patrol members.
- Represent the patrol at patrols leaders' council meetings when the patrol leader cannot attend.
- Set a good example.
- Wear the uniform correctly.
- Live by the Scout Oath and Law.
- Show Scout spirit.

In addition, the assistant patrol leader may be given special assignments such as working on a patrol service project or assisting certain patrol members with their advancement.

Patrol Scribe

The scribe of a patrol keeps the log—a record of what goes on at each patrol meeting. It provides an accurate account of decisions made, assignments of responsibilities, and patrol plans for upcoming events. To refresh everyone's memory at the beginning of a patrol meeting, the scribe may read the most recent log entry.

The scribe checks attendance, collects and records dues, and manages the budgets for outings. He may also be the patrol's Internet webmaster, encouraging patrol members to use e-mail to communicate with one another between meetings.

As you consider the candidates for patrol scribe, keep in mind that the task will be best suited to someone who has good writing skills, is well organized, and is dependable.

Patrol Quartermaster

The patrol quartermaster is responsible for the patrol equipment. He maintains inventory of all of the patrol gear and makes sure it is clean and ready for the patrol to use. If an item is broken, he repairs it if he can; if he can't, he brings it to the attention of the patrol leader. If the patrol has a chuck box for its frontcountry camp kitchen, the quartermaster can monitor its contents and see that it is fully stocked with cook gear and staple items. He checks out the gear for campouts and other patrol outings, and he makes sure everything is returned and properly stored afterward.

The responsibilities of the quartermaster are suited for a Scout who is organized, dependable, and aware of details.

Patrol Grubmaster

The grubmaster of a patrol takes the lead in planning menus for hikes and campouts. Of course, everyone in the patrol has a say in what he would like to eat. The grubmaster helps make those wishes into reality by writing out the menu, itemizing the ingredients, ensuring that purchases are made, and supervising food repackaging before a trip. Scouts who are completing advancement requirements for cooking can work closely with the grubmaster.

The grubmaster should be a Scout who is familiar with the cooking chapter of *The Boy Scout Handbook* and is aware of the importance of good nutrition. It will help if he is also good at math and measurements.

Patrol Cheermaster

The cheermaster leads the patrol in yells, songs, and skits. His is a vital role when the patrol is taking part in campfire programs. Just as important can be his contributions to patrol spirit during long hikes, when the weather on a camping trip turns stormy, or when the patrol is challenged by adversity. He should be an upbeat, outgoing person who can get up in front of a group and lead a song or a cheer.

Guidelines for Filling Patrol Leadership Positions

The following pointers will help guide your thinking as you set about the task of filling these positions:

- Take all the time you need to consider the responsibilities of each position and the qualifications of each patrol member, then make the right match. These positions do not need to be filled immediately.

- Be fair to all patrol members. Consider each Scout's advancement record, Scout spirit, and commitment to the patrol and troop. Take into account each patrol member's strengths, weaknesses, experience, and service to Scouting.

- Do not allow friendships with certain patrol members to interfere with your efforts to select the best person for each position.

- Discuss your ideas with the Scoutmaster or an assistant Scoutmaster.

Slicing Up the Leadership Pie

Leadership can be a bit like eating apple pie; eat an entire pie by yourself and there will be none left to share with anyone else. Chances are you will get a stomachache, too.

Cut that pie into pieces and give each patrol member a slice, though, and everyone can enjoy it and will come away from the experience feeling good about the whole thing.

As a patrol leader, you may be tempted to do everything by yourself. That's going to make you weary before long, and you may get a headache, too. On the other hand, if you spread the tasks of the patrol around fairly, each patrol member will feel that he has a real stake in the success of the group and you won't feel overwhelmed by a long list of tasks to be done.

Other Patrol Positions

The key leadership positions within a patrol are designed to ensure that the patrol will operate smoothly and that a number of patrol members will share in the responsibilities of planning and carrying out the patrol's meetings and activities.

In addition, there are many other opportunities for patrol members to pitch in and help complete a project, correct a problem, and lend a hand to others. For example, maintaining the stoves on a campout, cooking the meals, and cleaning up afterward are tasks that must be done if the patrol is to succeed. Patrol members can do their share, dividing up the work and passing around the responsibilities so that everyone has an equal chance to take on each task. With the guidance of the patrol leader, patrol members can develop a duty roster that outlines who does what, and when.

BSA Youth Leader Training Resources

Scouting takes pride in giving its youth leaders exciting, effective training. As a patrol leader, you will have opportunities to participate in some or all of these leadership offerings.

Introduction to Leadership

This is the first step of leadership training. The Scoutmaster will conduct it within a few days after you are elected to be senior patrol leader. Lasting not more than an hour, it will cover your responsibilities as senior patrol leader and upcoming events in the troop.

Troop Leadership Training

A three-module, three-hour training conference conducted by you and the Scoutmaster, Troop Leadership Training will reinforce the patrol method and encourage members of the patrol leader's council to set goals for their patrols and the troop.

National Youth Leadership Training

Many local councils throughout the country offer a weeklong youth leadership training. Conducted in the outdoor settings of council camps, these courses supplement training done within a troop and introduce senior patrol leaders and patrol leaders to more advanced leadership skills.

National Youth Leadership Instructor Camp and Advanced National Youth Leadership Experience

The BSA's National Council hosts National Youth Leadership Instructor Camp and/or Advanced National Youth Leadership Experience during the summer at Philmont Training Center. NYLIC prepares participants to conduct their council National Youth Leadership Training courses. NAYLE is a scenario course that allows participants to apply NYLT leadership skills in a wilderness environment. Participants must have completed the council National Youth Leadership Training and be nominated by the Scout executives of their local councils.

National Leadership Seminars

The Order of the Arrow hosts National Leadership Seminars focusing on the skills and attributes of leadership. Youth leaders invited to attend these weekend events must be at least 15 years of age or be serving as officers in their council's Order of the Arrow lodge.

Other Resources for Patrol Leaders

Scouting will provide many resources you can use as you fulfill your patrol leader responsibilities. For guidance and support, you can count on the senior patrol leader, Scoutmaster, assistant Scoutmasters, and members of the troop committee. A wealth of BSA literature contains information to help you make the most of your patrol and of your experience in Scouting. The following publications are of special interest to patrol leaders:

- *Boy Scout Handbook,* No. 33105
- *Boy Scout Requirements* (current year), No. 33215
- *Troop Program Resources,* No. 33588
- *Troop Program Features, Volumes I, II, and III,* Nos. 33110, 33111, 33112
- Troop Planning Work Sheet (from *Troop Program Features*)
- Troop Leadership Training Modules, No. 34306
- *Fieldbook,* No. 33104
- *Boys' Life* magazines
- *Boy Scout Songbook,* No. 33224A
- Troop and patrol rosters
- Copies of troop rules and policies
- Activity calendar (troop, district, council, chartered organization)
- First Class First Year Tracking Sheet, No. 34118A
- Campfire Program Planner Sheet, No. 33696
- BSA Supply catalog

In Conclusion

This book began by congratulating you on having accepted one of the best positions in Scouting—patrol leader. Eventually the time will come when you will have completed your term of office and will pass leadership of the patrol to someone else. When that happens,

you should be able to look back with pride at all that you and the patrol members have accomplished while you were wearing the patrol leader's patch.

No doubt the patrol will have become stronger because you were there. Certainly you and the other members of the patrol will have memories of lots of fine adventures and other Scouting activities. Together, you will have met many challenges and will have worked as a team to find solutions to all sorts of situations.

Scouting will present you with other leadership opportunities, both as a youth and as a young adult. Though you may no longer be a part of it, the patrol will continue to grow and thrive, building on the strong foundation you will have left and bringing in the fresh ideas and energy of new patrol leaders and new members.

You also will find that the leadership skills you learn as a patrol leader are going to serve you well in school, in your community, and in other settings beyond the BSA. By asking you to accept the responsibility for guiding a patrol, Scouting gives you hands-on opportunities to learn and practice essential methods of leading people. Wherever you go in life and whatever you do, those skills will go with you. Time and time again they are going to help you make a real difference in your life and in the lives of others.

Acknowledgments

The Boy Scouts of America gratefully acknowledges the contributions of the following people for their help in the preparing of *The Patrol Leader Handbook*.

- Scouts and Scouters throughout the country who participated in focus groups, photography efforts, and manuscript reviews
- Members of the National Council's Literature Review Committee: Bob Longoria, chairman; Jim Grossman; Mike O'Quinn; Larry Warlick

National Office Publishing Team

Project director
Joe C. Glasscock, Boy Scout Division, BSA

Account executive
Maria C. Dahl, Custom Communication Division, BSA

Author
Robert Birkby, Eagle Scout and mountaineer

Editor/copy editor
Beth McPherson, Custom Communication Division, BSA

Proofreader
Karen M. Kraft, Custom Communication Division, BSA

Design/art direction
Julie Moore, managing designer/art director;
  Custom Communication Division, BSA

Glenn Howard, assistant art director

Imaging artist
Melinda VanLone, Custom Communication Division, BSA

Prepress specialist
Joanne McGuire, Custom Communication Division, BSA

Print coordinator
Kimberly Kailey, Custom Communication Division, BSA

Photography
Michael Roytek, photography manager;
  Custom Communication Division, BSA

Randy Piland, freelance photographer

Kellie Pence, photography assistant;
  Custom Communication Division, BSA

Notes

Notes

Notes

Notes

Notes